RAIL ROVER
EAST MIDLANDS ROVER

John Jackson

AMBERLEY

First published 2021

Amberley Publishing
The Hill, Stroud
Gloucestershire, GL5 4EP

www.amberley-books.com

ISBN 978 1 4456 9016 2 (print)
ISBN 978 1 4456 9017 9 (ebook)

British Library Cataloguing in Publication Data.
A catalogue record for this book is available from
the British Library.

Typesetting by Aura Technology and Software
Services, India. Printed in the UK.

Contents

Introduction

For as long as I can remember, enthusiasts and railway lovers have taken advantage of rover tickets. Although they are a little marketed product offered, perhaps reluctantly, by today's railway operators, rover tickets continue to offer a flexible and attractively priced product for rail enthusiasts.

It was approaching fifty years ago that I had my first experience of these rail tickets in the 'ranger' and 'rover' series, including the 'big daddy' of them all, the All Line Rover. This ticket enables travel on virtually all of the whole UK railway network.

Such rover tickets have long been seen as a flexible way of travelling around a particular area of the country for a relatively low daily rate, particularly when compared with travelling using conventional day return ticket options. The privatisation of our railways has only added to the ticket's attraction, as the ticket places little restriction on which railway company's trains can be used within the ticket area.

This book in no way attempts to list the terms and conditions that apply to such tickets. Suffice to say that rovers are off peak tickets, generally available for travel after 09.00 Mondays to Fridays and anytime at weekends and on bank holidays. An internet search of 'GB Rail Rovers' will give the reader all the details that he or she may need.

Ironically, the 'go anywhere' All Line Rover ticket now has some additional restrictions. For example, the ticket has additional time travel constraints from both my local stations of Bedford and Milton Keynes Central. I can't join or alight at these stations before 10.00! For many (me included), the removal of most overnight services has also impacted on that All Line ticket's flexibility. Many of these overnight services offered passenger seating accommodation as well as sleeper berths.

I remember in the 1960s and 1970s the various cross-country options that enabled the enthusiast to end one day at one end of the country and travel to another for an early start the following day. Overnight travel from Brighton to Manchester and Newcastle to Bristol, avoiding crossing London, were just two of these well used options.

In this book it is, however, one of the UK's regional offerings that is the focus of the pages that follow. To use the rail industry's terminology, and not mine, let's explore the area covered by the East Midlands Rover ticket. Specifically, two weekly tickets are offered valid either for all seven days' travel or any three days of the purchaser's choice within the seven-day period. As a footnote, a ticket valid for one day only can also be purchased. Confusingly, the 'East Midlands Day Ranger' covers a different geographical area and is therefore ignored here.

A day's travel in the area covered by weekly East Midlands Rover tickets, factoring in the use of a railcard, works out currently at around £11 per day for each day of the full seven day ticket, and around £20 per day if using the '3 day in 7' option. Without a railcard the figures increase to £17 and just over £30 respectively. These calculations are based on 2019 prices.

So, let's take a look at the area that this ticket covers. It is a geographical area offering stark contrasts, from the peace and tranquillity of the Derbyshire Dales to the seaside at Skegness and Cleethorpes. At its very heart lies industrial towns and cities all seeking to diversify now that much of their industry has gone. Indeed, my schoolboy geography lessons remind me that this heartland was once dubbed the Yorkshire, Nottinghamshire and Derbyshire coalfield.

The ticket's area of validity extends from New Mills Central, Stoke-on-Trent and Stafford in the west to Cleethorpes and Skegness in the east, and from Meadowhall and Doncaster in the north to Bletchley in the south and encompasses Sheffield, Derby, Nottingham, Coventry, Rugby, Leicester and Peterborough.

And it's an area rich in diversity for the rail enthusiast, too. For this reason, I have divided the publication into a number of chapters each spotlighting the variety on offer.

This diversity therefore gives the East Midlands Rover ticket user a variety of options, including the chance to travel on lengthy stretches of all three of the country's main north-to-south arteries, namely the West Coast Main Line, Midland Main Line and East Coast Main Line. This gives the traveller the opportunity to enjoy, for example, a frequent, high speed run on an 80-mile stretch of the East Coast Main Line between Doncaster and Peterborough. The Midland Main Line offers a greater distance with around 100 miles between Bedford and Sheffield covered by the ticket, although currently a change of train at Leicester would be necessary to achieve this.

Notable exclusions that fall outside its boundaries are all Birmingham stations, including New Street, and the railway centre of Crewe.

This means that this rover ticket includes many of the rail stations in the centre of England that see the greatest number and wide variety of freight trains on offer on today's railways. This is despite the area seeing a dramatic downturn in coal movements in a region that was once rich in both coal mines and coal-burning power stations. Today, much of that coal traffic has given way to other freight movements, such as containers and aggregates. Much of the rail freight traffic from the UK's two main container ports, Felixstowe and Southampton, passes through this rover ticket's area. Add to this the importance of the counties of Leicestershire and Derbyshire for their stone quarrying and there's still much for the freight train lover to enjoy.

The UK passenger railway continues to evolve following privatisation in the 1990s. The services are now in the hands of private operators within a franchise structure. This includes a role for the government, too, when commercial enterprise fails to deliver on commitments.

This franchise system is a changing, if not a volatile, marketplace. Space precludes me including a history of all the players who have operated in this East Midlands area over the last quarter of a century. At present, I calculate that ten different franchises (or brands) are offered in the area; several of these are owned by the same parent company. Suffice to say, these tickets are valid on all but two of these operators' services as far as I am aware. The only exceptions being Grand Central and, perhaps not surprisingly, Caledonian Sleeper.

Perhaps, then, it is the wide variety of passenger and freight traffic on offer across the area that appeals to me as a regular rail traveller. Since swapping the rat race for the rail tracks at the turn of the millennium, I have made use of literally hundreds of these weekly tickets. In this publication, I have selected all the photos while using these East Midlands Rover tickets as a rail traveller.

All the photos chosen have been taken on railway station platforms, or a short walk from the station entrances. There are a number of strategic rail locations that fall within this area that are not directly accessed by rail. For example, I am thinking of the rail lines around Toton, on the Derbyshire and Nottinghamshire border, which lie at the very heart of this region. Toton bank is a popular venue for rail enthusiasts, me included, but best accessed by car. Alternatively, the public transport user would reach Toton by tram or bus, and then onwards on foot, and is therefore excluded from the scope of this publication.

Our journey around the area broadly takes us in a clockwise direction commencing our journey in the south-west corner, around Bletchley and Milton Keynes. The contents page shows the sequence that I've used thereafter. A map showing the full area covered by this ticket appears before the photo section.

Finally, I hope you enjoy your journey through the pages that follow as much as I have enjoyed compiling them.

John Jackson

East Midlands Rover – Area of Validity

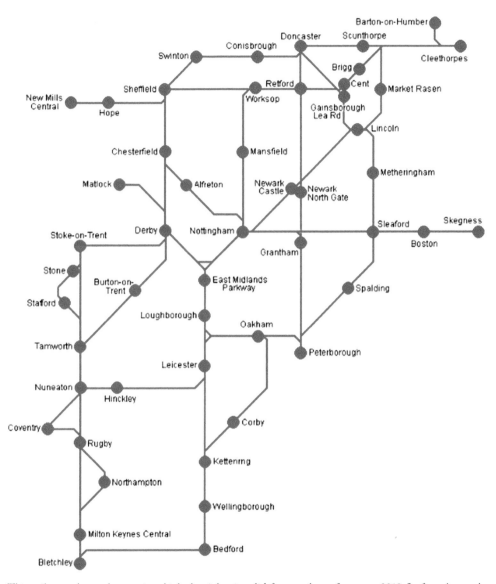

This rail map shows the area in which the ticket is valid for travel, as of autumn 2019. In fact, the area's boundaries have changed little, if at all, for as long as I can remember.

Around Bletchley and Milton Keynes

Our photographic journey round the rover ticket area starts at Bletchley, on the West Coast Main Line (WCML), in the south-west corner of its area of validity. On 24 May 2017, a three-loco convoy is seen approaching Bletchley on a Crewe to Wembley light engine move. No. 92028 is seen leading No. 66703 *Doncaster PSB 1981–2002* and No. 90042.

The city of Milton Keynes was the biggest of a series of new towns created in the 1960s. Located around 50 miles from London, it enjoys a fast and frequent service both southward to the capital and to a number of key destinations further north. On 28 August 2018, nine coach Pendolino No. 390006 calls at the city's Central station on a service then operated by Virgin Trains.

The town of Wolverton lies on the northern edge of the city of Milton Keynes. On 22 September 2012, No. 67026 *Diamond Jubilee* passes southbound through one of Wolverton's platforms on another Crewe to Wembley light engine move.

The town of Wolverton has a long association with the railways, housing workshops that date back to the 1830s. These shops are proud to be the home of the Royal Train coaching stock. On 23 March 2017, 'royal' loco No. 67005 *Queen's Messenger* passes through Milton Keynes Central on a rake of empty stock returning to their Wolverton base. The loco is on the rear, with a sister Class 67 loco leading.

The Wolverton workshops continue to maintain a wide variety of other items of rolling stock. On 26 June 2015, a pair of Class 90 locos, No. 90037 *Spirit of Dagenham* and No. 90014 *Norfolk and Norwich Festival*, have made a stop there to pick up a single coach and return it to Greater Anglia at Norwich. The train is seen passing Bletchley.

Another empty stock move on 9 September 2019 saw new London Overground unit No. 710107 pause at Milton Keynes Central while working, under its own power, from Ilford to Crewe.

This southern end of the WCML sees a variety of freight traffic. On 5 March 2018, a pair of Freightliner's electric loco stalwarts, Nos 86609 and 86610, head north through Bletchley on a container working from Felixstowe to Trafford Park, Manchester. Both locos continue to see revenue-earning service despite being built in 1965.

Heading in the opposite direction on 26 October 2017, No. 70011 heads another liner through Milton Keynes Central station. This time the working is from Crewe to Felixstowe. By contrast, the company's small fleet of Class 70 locos date from 2009, with No. 70011 itself being delivered via Newport Docks in January 2011.

Virtually all the non-passenger traffic takes the Northampton loop line at Hanslope Junction and rejoins the WCML near Rugby. Daventry International Rail Freight Terminal (DIRFT) is located on this loop line. On 10 January 2018, No. 66142 heads through Northampton on a southbound train of empty vans from DIRFT to the Channel Tunnel at Dollands Moor.

Northampton is also the location of this delayed freight train on 4 April 2006. In a scene that's unlikely to be repeated, No. 60078 leads No. 60053 *Nordic Terminal*, which had failed earlier. The pair are seen on the now very late running service from Peak Forest, in Derbyshire, to Bletchley. This working, then in the hands of EWS, is at present in the hands of GB Railfreight (GBRf).

Milton Keynes Central is the northern terminus of a service from East Croydon operated by Southern. On 15 October 2015, No. 377702 has just terminated on an inbound working. The unit will return south shortly, skirting Central London by way of Kensington Olympia and then Clapham Junction.

An electric unit working of a different kind sees four-car Class 325 units, often in multiple, working for Royal Mail traffic between London, Warrington and Shieldmuir, near Glasgow. On 20 August 2016, No. 325016 leads a twelve-coach service through Central station on a northbound service.

Bletchley is also the current terminus of the Marston Vale service from Bedford. On 11 December 2016, these services were in the hands of Class 150 and 153 units. On that afternoon, Nos 150105 and 153354 are seen in the branch platforms. The Class 150 unit will form the 14.01 to Bedford after a set swap.

These units have recently been replaced by a fleet of three Class 230 units converted from former London Underground stock by Viva Rail. Two of these units, Nos 230003 and 230004, were to be found side by side at Bletchley on 9 September 2019. Viva Rail have converted these units from former London Underground stock, originally built by Metro-Cammell, in the early 1980s.

The rover ticket permits travel along the 16-mile Marston Vale branch between Bletchley and Bedford. On 24 May 2017, No. 150109 makes a call at Fenny Stratford station's single platform.

The branch also offers non-passenger traffic a route between the WCML and the Midland Main Line. On 15 February 2018, Nos 47813, 56303 and 47812 are waiting for the signal to take the Bedford branch out of Bletchley on a light engine move to Leicester.

Rugby and Coventry

The railway around Rugby has seen a great deal of change in the days since privatisation, with the station virtually completely rebuilt and tracks realigned. On 19 June 2017, eleven-coach Pendolino, No. 390126 *Virgin Enterprise*, heads north through Rugby on a non-stop Virgin Trains service.

Semi-fast services are in the hands of London Northwestern Railways. They have a large fleet of Class 350 units, including No. 350231 seen in their new livery on 11 February 2019. The unit calls at Rugby on a service from London Euston to Birmingham New Street via Northampton.

Since the introduction of the Pendolino fleet, Rugby has been the base for a rescue loco, commonly referred to as a 'Thunderbird', in the event of a rare failure. On 29 March 2018, No. 57304 *Pride of Cheshire* stands in Rugby's south bay awaiting a possible call.

There was a very different look to the station in this view of the bay platforms on 28 April 1994, around the time of rail privatisation. Class 31 loco, No. 31467, sports the familiar BR blue colours of that era as it awaits its next Infrastructure duties.

A few years later, on 11 March 2000, No. 47784 *Condover Hall* stands in one of the north bay platforms, still carrying Rail Express Systems colours. These north-facing bay platforms have since been removed.

This view, from the top of Rugby station's multi-storey car park, shows the stabling opportunities at the south end today. On 11 July 2017, No. 88008 *Ariadne*, No. 86259 *Peter Pan* and No. 57311 *Thunderbird* are all stabled.

The loco-hauled movement of units around the country often involves use of the West Coast Main Line (WCML). On 11 July 2017, No. 37884 hauls No. 319012 and No. 319215 through Rugby on a move from Hornsey depot in North London to Long Marston for storage.

On 10 June 2016, No. 90044 waits at Rugby while hauling a Crewe to Felixstowe freightliner. It will take the Northampton loop on its journey south, booked to follow a local passenger service.

On 13 July 2013, Freightliner's No. 66550 is taking a circuitous route hauling its rake of wagons from Willesden, North London, to the Leicestershire quarry at Stud Farm. It will take the Coventry line from here at Rugby, and then via the West Midlands.

At the time of rail privatisation, the West Midlands enjoyed regular loco-hauled services on the flagship service to London Euston. On 28 September 1993, Class 86 electric loco, No. 86213 *Lancashire Witch*, is seen calling at Coventry while propelling its London-bound service from Wolverhampton.

Nowadays, CrossCountry Voyagers are regularly seen at Coventry on a variety of passenger services. On 21 May 2017, No. 221102 *John Cabot* calls on a Virgin Trains service to London Euston.

Two years earlier, on 15 October 2015, another Voyager, No. 221135, calls at Coventry on a CrossCountry Trains service from Manchester Piccadilly. It will take the Leamington Spa line on a service to Bournemouth, via Reading and Southampton.

The local passenger service from Coventry to Kenilworth and Leamington Spa was reintroduced in 2018. On 9 May that year, single-car unit No. 153354 waits at Coventry to form a local service to Leamington just a few days after the service finally commenced.

The majority of West Midlands stopping services are now in the hands of Class 350 units. On 7 July 2014, No. 350262 calls at Coventry on a service from Birmingham New Street to Northampton. On arrival at Northampton, further coaches will be added for the onward journey to London Euston.

The route from Nuneaton through Coventry to Leamington is used by numerous freight trains, particularly those heading to and from Southampton Docks. On 9 May 2017, Freightliner's No. 66951 has No. 66502 *Basford Hall Centenary 2001* for company as the pair thread their way across Coventry's main running lines on a Crewe to Southampton container train.

Less common on the Leamington line was the appearance of a West Coast Railway Company (WCRC) Class 33 on 14 December 2017. Together with a Class 47 loco, No. 47245, this WCRC pairing was taking two of their coaches from Eastleigh to their base at Carnforth.

Stafford

The town of Stafford lies at an important junction where the West Coast Main Lines from the Trent Valley and the West Midlands converge. Long-distance services from London Euston on both routes have been handled by Pendolinos since the beginning of the twenty-first century. On 21 March 2016, No. 390107 *Independence Day Resergence*, on the right, and No. 390042 *City of Bangor/Dinas Bangor* are seen passing through Stafford at speed.

The Pendolinos replaced the popular loco-hauled services that had seen in the privatisation of our railways. On 28 October 1993, No. 90010 calls at Stafford. The InterCity liveried electric loco remains in passenger service on the London Liverpool Street to Norwich route.

A wide variety of freight operators' workings can be seen at Stafford during the course of an average day, making it a popular choice for today's rail enthusiasts. On 4 May 2017, DB Cargo's No. 66005 is seen passing south through the station on a Halewood to Southampton car train.

Some of DB Cargo's Anglo Scottish freight services are handled by pairs of their Class 90 electric locos. On 8 June 2016, No. 90036 *Driver Jack Mills* leads No. 90028 on a southbound container train from Mossend, near Glasgow to Daventry.

Freightliner often uses its WCML container trains as a chance to move locos between its traction bases at Ipswich and Crewe for servicing purposes. On 8 June 2016, No. 90045 hitches a lift as it is tucked in behind Nos 86637 and 86614 on a Felixstowe to Crewe service.

In this view at Rugeley Trent Valley, a few miles south of Stafford, it's the turn of No. 66546 to be conveyed by No. 90046 within this northbound freightliner service from Felixstowe to Ditton, Merseyside.

On the same day, 18 July 2016, London Midland diesel unit No. 170503 is seen at Rugeley having arrived on a service from Birmingham New Street via Cannock. Electrification of this line has seen these diesel units displaced by Class 350 electric units.

Other operators' electric units are often scene clocking up the mileage on the WCML before entering service elsewhere. On 24 March 2017, Great Western Railways' electric units Nos 387146 and 387147 are heading south on a Crewe to Wembley run.

Direct Rail Services (DRS) also operate Anglo Scottish container trains. In 2014, these services were operated by Class 66 locos, such as No. 66422 on 8 December that year, on a Daventry to Grangemouth service. These trains are currently handled by Class 88s.

GBRf workings are also seen through Stafford. On 28 June 2017, No. 66711 *Sence* is seen on an Infrastructure working from Toton to Crewe. It will return later with a more demanding load moving in the opposite direction.

Colas Rail locos are less common. On 3 June 2014, one of their Class 70 locos, No. 70810, is seen heading south through the station on a light engine move from Seaforth, Merseyside to the West Midlands yard at Bescot, near Walsall.

Class 92 locos have also been used on Anglo Scottish container trains in the past. On 27 August 2014, No. 92039 *Johann Strauss* heads south on a Mossend to Daventry working.

DRS handle the British Nuclear flask traffic between their base at Sellafield, Cumbria and several locations around the UK. One such working which ran for a number of years was that to and from Bridgwater in Somerset. On 8 June 2016, Nos 37605 and 37612 head north through the station.

By 28 June 2017, these veteran Class 37s had given way in favour of pairs of Class 68 locos. In thankfully better weather, No. 68001 *Evolution* and No. 68030 head north on a similar working.

This stretch of the WCML often sees one-off moves for a variety of operators. On 22 September 2017, Class 50 diesel loco No. 50008 *Thunderer* was used for route-learning duties and is seen about to leave Stafford for Derby.

On 9 March 2018, Rail Operations Group loco No. 37884 is seen on another one-off light engine move. It was called upon to drag a pair of DRS Class 68s on a Wembley to Crewe light engine move. Both locos, No. 68019 *Brutus* and No. 68021 *Tireless*, carry the First Trans Pennine Express livery and have just started to see work on that company's Liverpool to Scarborough services.

Nuneaton, Tamworth and Burton on Trent

This triangle of towns in the centre of England encompass the busy lines of the WCML and cross-country routes between Birmingham and Derby and Birmingham to Leicester. As a result, they are among the busiest for freight trains on today's railway. On 3 June 2019, DB Cargo's No. 60059 *Swinden Dalesman* heads through the High Level platforms at Tamworth with a loaded aviation fuel tank working from Lindsey on Humberside to the nearby facility at Kingsbury.

Heading in the opposite direction on 24 November 2014, Freightliner's No. 66527 approaches Tamworth High Level with an empty coal hopper working from Rugeley to Barnetby, South Humberside. This once familiar sight of a coal train is fast being consigned to history. The loco has since been shipped to Poland.

On 13 April 2016, Colas Rail's No. 56302 is about to pass through Tamworth High Level. It had charge of the company's working between Washwood Heath in Birmingham and Boston Docks in Lincolnshire.

The WCML platforms are located at the lower level at Tamworth. On 11 March 2016, a pair of new electric units, Nos 387215 and 387217, pass the Low Level platforms on a Crewe to Wembley mileage accumulation run for Gatwick Express.

In the early twenty-first century, Tamworth Low Level's stopping services along the Trent Valley were in the hands of single-car Class 153 diesel units. They were both unreliable and little used. Only one passenger has alighted from this afternoon working by Central Trains' No. 153381 on 3 September 2002.

In contrast, on 6 February 2017 four-car Class 350 electric unit No. 350106 calls on the hourly Trent Valley stopping service which has now been extended to London Euston. These service improvements have paid off. Custom has now increased sufficiently for most of these services to be formed of eight coaches.

12 miles to the south-east of Tamworth lies the equally busy station at Nuneaton. On 15 October 2019, DB Cargo's No. 66185 *DP World London Gateway* heads south on an intermodal service from Trafford Park, Manchester, to London Gateway. The platforms and tracks on the right carry the Leicester to Birmingham line across the WCML.

On 10 April 2018, West Cost Railway Company's (WCRC) No. 57601 heads in the opposite direction on a northbound empty coaching stock working. These WCRC workings link their stabling points at Southall in West London with Carnforth, near Lancaster.

On 9 January 2017, DRS Class 37 No. 37605 heads through Nuneaton on a light engine move to return it from use in Norwich to its home depot at Gresty Bridge in Crewe. The loco had been routed across country via Peterborough and Leicester.

On 3 September 2018, another light engine move sees a pair of locos heading south from Crewe to Wembley. The Class 59, No. 59005 *Kenneth J Painter*, is leading No. 67024 and will return to its Mendip stone duties after servicing at Crewe.

By 16 August 2019, local services from Nuneaton to Coventry had been extended to Leamington Spa and the single Class 153 units displaced from the branch. Two-car Class 172 units, such as No. 172005 seen here awaiting departure, are now used on this service. They have transferred from Gospel Oak services in East London, following electrification of the line there.

Burton on Trent station is managed by East Midlands Railway, although passenger services are in the hands of CrossCountry Trains. Class 170 units provide a half-hourly service, such as this two-car example, No. 170116, calling on 23 May 2016 while on a Nottingham to Cardiff Central working.

This half hourly CrossCountry Trains service is augmented with a handful of high-speed train workings between the North East and the South West. On 8 February 2019, power car No. 43357 is on the rear of a working bound for Plymouth.

On the same day, a pair of DB Cargo Class 66s, Nos 66137 and 66088, lead the regular Infrastructure working between the yards at Bescot and Toton, on the Derbyshire and Nottinghamshire border. This particular working is now in the hands of GB Railfreight.

Freightliner has commenced applying a revised livery to its loco fleet since becoming a subsidiary of Genesee & Wyoming. On 8 February 2019, No. 66413 *Lest We Forget* sports this new livery as it heads through Burton on Trent on a cement working from Earles Sidings, near Hope in Derbyshire, to the terminal at Walsall.

Just to the north of the station at Burton on Trent lies the rail complex of Nemesis Rail. This location often accounts for loco moves through Burton station as a result. On 14 July 2017, a trio of light engines pass through on a DRS working from Crewe to Nemesis at Burton. The convoy is led by No. 57306 *Her Majesty's Railway Inspectorate 175* with Nos 37602 and 37606. The latter loco is nearest the camera as the convoy makes a brief pause alongside the station platform.

Derby and Nottingham

The two cities of Derby and Nottingham lie at the centre of the rover ticket area. From Derby, East Midlands Railway (EMR) operate an hourly service to Stoke on Trent and Crewe. On 10 November 2014, single-car unit No. 153383 waits to form an afternoon departure for Crewe.

Derby to Crewe services have, in more recent times, often been formed of two-car units. On 16 February 2016, No. 158806 forms the 10.42 service to Crewe. The rover ticket is valid on these services as far as Stoke on Trent.

For many years, London Underground (LUL) stock regularly emerged from the nearby workshops at Derby Litchurch Lane. These were invariably moved by four Class 20s working in multiple; two either end of the unit and barrier vehicles. On 15 November 2016, Nos 20107 and 20096, with Nos 20314 and 20905 at the far end, wait to take their barriers into the works to collect an LUL train.

A similar contract is in place to move newly constructed Crossrail units between Derby and the test track at Old Dalby, and on delivery to the London depot at Old Oak. On 20 September 2017, No. 345017 awaits a move to the Old Dalby test track. Track improvement work within the station area has seen a new platform built on the site where the unit is stabled.

On 12 February 2015, old and new DRS locos worked through Derby on a light engine move. Almost fifty years separates the construction date of Class 37 loco, No. 37423 *Spirit of The Lakes*, built in 1965, seen in the company of Class 68 loco, No. 68001 *Evolution*, built in 2014. The pair are working from Crewe to Barrow Hill, near Chesterfield.

On 3 June 2015, DC Rail Class 56 loco, No. 56103, is seen in the Derby station area with a rake of empty box wagons on a move from nearby Chaddesden sidings to Stockton on Tees.

Most of the freight traffic passing through this part of the East Midlands takes the line that bisects Derby and Nottingham, namely the Erewash Valley route through the significant yards at Toton. One regular exception that works through Derby station is the GBRf working from Tinsley, Sheffield, to the Leicestershire quarry at Bardon Hill. On 8 July 2016, No. 66761 *Wensleydale Railway Association 25 Years 1990–2015* is seen on this working.

Another working that has been routed through Derby for a number of years is the empty steel wagon working returning from Wolverhampton to Immingham, Humberside. On 11 October 2019, No. 60040 *The Territorial Army Centenary* is in charge of this service.

The Derby area has a long historical association with coal traffic, although these days the sight of such traffic is rare. On 12 February 2015, Freightliner's No. 66604 takes a rake of empty coal hoppers north through Derby station. The loco is working from the now closed power station at Rugeley to Midland Road in Leeds.

Twenty years earlier, shortly after privatisation, Class 58 loco No. 58004 takes a rake of iconic 'Merry Go Round' coal hoppers through Derby. The date is 17 October 1997. Over 11,000 of these coal hoppers were used on the UK coal traffic from the mid 1960s.

Throughout the day, Nottingham has two passenger trains an hour to London St Pancras International operated by EMR; one worked by an HST and the other by a Meridian. On 15 August 2019, five-car Meridian No. 222008 *Derby Etches Park* waits to form a St Pancras service. On the right is CrossCountry Trains unit No. 170114 waiting to head to Birmingham New Street.

The East Midlands Trains franchise changed hands in 2019, with Stagecoach-operated EMT giving way to East Midlands Railway. To mark the end of eleven years of EMT operation, HST car No. 43081 was chosen to carry vinyl marking the occasion. It is seen on 15 August 2019 waiting to leave for London.

Nottingham sees a variety of workings for diesel multiple units with the Lincolnshire seaside resort of Skegness being a popular destination, particularly in the summer months. On 27 January 2016, EMT's No. 156410 waits in the Skegness bay platform on one such service.

The city of Nottingham also enjoys an hourly service to Leeds via Sheffield and Barnsley. Operated by Northern, their Class 158s have been the mainstay on these services for many years. On 2 August 2019, No. 158905 is waiting to leave on a morning service to Leeds.

Chesterfield

This Derbyshire town lies at the convergence of routes north from both Nottingham and Derby, as well as the freight route from Toton northwards. On 16 February 2018, EMT's Meridian No. 222008 *Derby Etches Park* is seen on a southbound service alongside CrossCountry Trains' Voyager No. 221127 on a northbound working.

EMR's London to Sheffield services are usually formed of five-car or seven-car Meridians. On 8 October 2019, however, four-car No. 222104 is pressed into service. It is the only example presently carrying the new franchisee's livery.

A number of former Scotrail Class 170 units were recently transferred to Northern by Arriva. One of these is seen through Chesterfield on 11 April 2018 on a Leeds Holbeck to Nottingham empty stock working.

The Class 170 transfers are linked to the introduction of short set HSTs in Scotland. On 7 August 2019, a pair of these power cars, Nos 43135 and 43126, is seen heading through the station on a move from Edinburgh's Craigentinny depot to the Brush workshops at Loughborough.

The nearby stately home at Chatsworth is a popular destination for charter train passengers, leaving and returning to their trains at Chesterfield station. These trains are usually worked by a pair of Class 67 locos, operating in top'n'tail mode. On 21 September 2017, No. 67013 is seen on the rear of a working from London King's Cross.

Another Class 67, No. 67029 *Royal Diamond*, is seen at Chesterfield on 7 September 2012. This time it is operating the train reserved exclusively for the management of DB Cargo and company guests. The stock for this occasionally used service is stabled and maintained at Toton.

The nearby Barrow Hill complex brings occasional loco movements to the Chesterfield station area. On 24 March 2014, a vintage trio of DRS locos is seen heading south on a light engine move from Barrow Hill to Crewe. Class 20 loco No. 20301, built in 1959, leads No. 37059, built in 1962, and No. 47501, built in 1966.

Chesterfield enjoys a variety of freight traffic, although the volume has reduced dramatically with the downturn in coal traffic. On 7 November 1995, Class 56 loco No. 56086 *The Magistrates' Association* passes the station on a northbound 'Merry Go Round' coal working.

Almost two decades later, on 17 July 2014, Freightliner's No. 66522 heads north through the station on a rake of Heavyhaul coal hoppers. The MGR wagons had by this date given way to a new generation of coal-carrying wagons in use with the now privately owned rail freight operators.

Colas Rail made use of these coal hoppers for a short-lived working into Ratcliffe Power Station, Nottinghamshire. On 11 February 2013, their Class 66 loco No. 66848 is seen on a UK Coal working to Ratcliffe from Wolsingham, on the Weardale Railway.

A number of steel-related freight flows continue to operate through Chesterfield. One long-standing working sees DB Cargo Class 66 head south on 8 June 2017 on a service carrying long welded rail from Scunthorpe to Eastleigh, near Southampton. The service is currently operated by GB Railfreight.

On 7 August 2019, DB Cargo Class 60 No. 60066 heads north through Chesterfield on the returning empty steel wagons from Wolverhampton to Immingham. The loco's livery promotes Drax Power Station.

Sheffield and the Hope Valley

The Yorkshire city is journey's end for most EMR services from London St Pancras International. On 14 January 2020, No. 222006 *The Carbon Cutter* has just terminated on a service from St Pancras.

Sheffield is also a stabling point for the Class 142 'Pacer' units. Although their days would appear to be finally numbered, the unit holding sides were home to Nos 142079, 142020 and 142091 as recently as 2 August 2019.

The Class 142 units were supported by Class 144s on local Northern services around Yorkshire. On 24 March 2016, two-car unit No. 144012 stands in one of Sheffield's bay platforms on a service to Leeds.

These diesel multiple units have worked in the Sheffield area since the last of their predecessors, the first-generation units, were withdrawn. One of the last of these to remain in service, No. 101677, is seen in the Hope Valley bay platform on 8 August 1996.

Northern single-car Class 153s are also regulars on local services, increasingly working in pairs. On 12 September 2019, Nos 153360 and 153380 have just terminated in Sheffield. The latter unit still carries its former Great Western Railway colours.

First Trans Pennine Express operate services between Manchester Airport and Cleethorpes. On 23 March 2015, unit No. 185108 is unusually stabled out of traffic in Sheffield station, following cancellation of its service beyond here to Cleethorpes.

The East Midlands Rover ticket offers travel as far west as New Mills Central, via Derbyshire's Hope Valley, by using Northern by Arriva's services. On 21 March 2018, Pacer unit No. 142048 calls at Edale on a stopping service to Sheffield.

The Class 150 is one of the unit classes to replace these Pacer units. On 3 April 2019, No. 150119 slows to call at Edale, also on a Sheffield-bound service. The unit is carrying the latest Northern by Arriva livery.

The Hope Valley line was handed a last-minute reprieve in the 1960s. Initially listed for closure under the Beeching proposals, it remained open at the expense of the alternative route between Sheffield and Manchester via Woodhead, which was closed instead. By the 1990s, Regional Railways provided a service on the route. On 14 August 1993, No. 158772 passes Edale station.

Twenty-five years later, the signal box at Edale and its semaphore signals are still in use. On 20 March 2018, No. 185139 passes on a First TransPennine Express service to Cleethorpes.

Class 170 units were still in use on some of these services on 22 March 2015, when No. 170303 was seen at Edale on the rear of a four-car working.

As already mentioned, the Class 150 units have become the preferred traction for Northern's local services on the route. On 21 March 2018, No. 150269 calls at Hope on its journey to Manchester Piccadilly.

The Hope Valley line's reprieve has meant that a number of freight trains can leave the quarries in this area at both the east and west ends of this line. On 1 April 2019, GB Railfreight's No. 66788 passes Edale on a rake of empty hoppers from Washwood Heath, Birmingham, to Peak Forest, near Buxton. The train will leave the Hope Valley at Chinley.

On 21 March 2018, Freightliner's No. 66518 is seen at Grindleford heading east to join the Midland Main Line at Dore, near Sheffield. It is heading to West Burton Power Station on a working from Earles Sidings, near Hope.

One of DB Cargo's long-standing workings in the area operates from Dowlow quarry to Ashbury's, Manchester. On 21 March 2018, No. 60015 is in charge as the train approaches Chinley station.

Freightliner light engine loco moves are common between their stabling point at Earles and the quarries around Buxton. On 20 March 2018, No. 66603 has just left Earles sidings and is seen passing Edale on a light engine move to Tunstead quarry.

Doncaster

The Yorkshire town of Doncaster occupies a pivotal position on the East Coast Main Line (ECML) and is the northern extremity of this rover ticket's validity. On 13 May 2013, Class 91 loco, No. 91111 is seen arriving on an ECML working, in the East Coast livery of the day. In 2014, this loco was chosen to receive a livery in memory of the men of regiments along the ECML who lost their lives in serving their country. The loco was named *For the Fallen* at the same time.

Much has happened to both the private operation and the traction used on the ECML since then. On 30 August 2019, LNER power car No. 43306 leads a northbound HST working non-stop through Doncaster's centre lines. The line's much loved HSTs have now been displaced.

LNER Azumas are the new order on ECML services to Leeds, Newcastle and Scotland. On 3 September 2019, No. 801105 heads south through Doncaster on a working to London King's Cross.

The hiring in of HST power cars from East Midlands Trains is now in the past. On 20 June 2019, No. 43061 calls at Doncaster while on the rear of a Leeds to King's Cross service. It is being passed by Class 180 unit No. 180101 on a Grand Central service from London to Sunderland.

Some of the LNER Class 91s are scheduled to remain in service for a few more months. There's a chance, then, that light engine moves such as this one could be repeated. On 13 February 2018, DB Cargo Class 90 No. 90034 drags both Nos 91105 and 91120 on a move to Doncaster from the North London depot at Bounds Green.

There will also be a requirement for Class 67 rescue locos, or 'Thunderbirds', for a little longer yet. One of the rescue bases for these locos is the West Yard adjacent to Doncaster station. On 3 September 2015, it's the turn of No. 67026 *Diamond Jubilee* to be stabled there on this duty.

The station platforms offer a view of both the West Yard and the adjacent workshops of Wabtec. On 17 July 2014, Wabtec-liveried diesel shunter No. 08669 *Bob Machin* shunts in West Yard.

Doncaster sees a wide variety of rolling stock moving to and from these Wabtec workshops. On 8 September 2016, Colas Rail's No. 47739 *Robin* of *Templecombe 1938–2013* has just worked in on one such completed move.

The West Yard has also been a stabling base for new Northern units on delivery and test. These include the Class 195s which commenced introduction to service during 2019. On 3 September that year, No. 195103 stands in the yard.

Introduction of new diesel and electric units will see a phasing out of Northern's older, life-expired stock. One of the most travelled classes of these units, the Class 322, has seen service across England and Scotland in the last thirty years. On 27 April 2016, No. 322481 waits at Doncaster forming a stopping service to Wakefield and Leeds.

Doncaster's West Yard is also used as a stabling point for the numerous Network Rail Test Trains that operate around the network. On 2 August 2019, DRS Class 68 loco No. 68009 *Titan* is stabled on one such duty.

Much of the freight traffic that once passed through Doncaster's platforms now uses avoiding lines in the area, with a noticeable reduction in volume across a typical day. On 5 July 2016, DB Cargo's No. 66095 heads north through the station on an Infrastructure working from Doncaster to Tyne Yard.

Light engine moves remain a common sight, with any of the main freight operators' locos candidates to make an appearance. On 6 January 2016, it's the turn of a pair of Colas Class 60s, No. 60021 and No. 60076 *Dunbar*. They are seen reversing in the station on a move from Doncaster Marshgate to Tyne Yard.

Back in 1992, the area would see an almost endless stream of coal trains. In readiness for their work in the week ahead, a convoy of Class 56s is heading for Doncaster Depot. On 3 August, a Monday, No. 56030 *Eggborough Power Station*, and Nos 56081, 56069 and 56082 are the locos involved.

Barnetby and Cleethorpes

Our journey around the East Midlands Rover ticket area now brings us to its north-eastern limit of validity, on South Humberside. First Trans Pennine service operate the longer distance services in the area with an hourly service linking Cleethorpes with Sheffield and Manchester. On 5 July 2018, No. 185109 approaches Barnetby station with a service to Manchester Airport.

Local services are in the hands of both Northern and East Midlands Railway. On 7 July 2018, Class 144 unit No. 144009 and Class 153 unit No. 153326 are in opposite platforms in this view from the station footbridge. The Class 144 unit offers a token services, with three trains running on Saturdays only, serving the stations at Brigg and Kirton Lindsey.

Barnetby station has long been popular with enthusiasts, not least because of the area's association with the Class 60 loco fleet. On 28 June 2018, Colas Rail's No. 60076 *Dunbar* approaches the station on the empty bitumen tanks returning from Preston to Lindsey.

DB Cargo's dwindling fleet of these locos still sees use on the numerous tank trains to and from the oil terminals at both Humber and Lindsey on South Humberside. On 3 May 2017, No. 60054 heads east through the station on a rake of empties from Kingsbury, near Tamworth.

The Colas Rail bitumen workings are more likely to see Class 56 or Class 70 haulage today, since their Class 60s have now been transferred to GB Railfreight. On 3 September 2019, it's the turn of No. 70816 to haul this working, seen as it approaches Barnetby.

Much has changed since this view of Barnetby, taken on 16 January 2016. Freightliner's Class 66 loco, No. 66549, passes the impressive array of semaphores and Barnetby East signal box on a loaded coal train from Immingham to Ratcliffe Power Station. The semaphore signals have now been replaced and Barnetby East signal box itself has been closed.

Freightliner now operate the regular flow of iron ore being moved between Immingham and the nearby ore terminal at Santon, Scunthorpe. On 12 July 2017, No. 66622 approaches Barnetby as it takes a rake of empty wagons back to Immingham.

Barnetby also sees a variety of steel traffic passing through the station. Early on Saturday 7 July 2018, DB Cargo's No. 66098 is nearing journey's end having left Margam in South Wales the previous evening. This view from the station footbridge, looking west towards Wrawby Junction, shows the colour light signals that have replaced the semaphores here.

Freightliner also handles the local coal traffic between Immingham and the coal handling plant at Scunthorpe. On 6 July 2018, No. 66613 passes Ulceby station on a loaded working bound for Scunthorpe. This station lies at the junction of the freight lines into the Immingham complex and the local passenger line to Barton–upon-Humber.

The rover ticket is valid on this Barton-upon-Humber branch, operated by a single unit operating to either Grimsby Town or Cleethorpes. On 6 July 2018, Northern's No. 153331 is seen departing New Holland on one such service.

In 2019 significant service improvements were promised for Grimsby Town station's passengers which could include through services to Nottingham and to London. Meantime, the service pattern remains mainly unchanged from when this photo was taken on 11 April 2012. It shows No. 153301 on a Barton-upon-Humber to Cleethorpes service.

The journey's end for First TransPennine Express services from Manchester Airport is at the seaside resort of Cleethorpes. On 6 July 2018, No. 185137 waits in Cleethorpes platform to return to Manchester. The beach and the Humber estuary are a few hundred yards to the right of this photo.

Lincoln and around Lincolnshire

The East Midlands Rover is valid throughout the county of Lincolnshire. It may be regarded as a railway backwater by many, but there are, thankfully, a number of Lincolnshire stations and lines that survived the area's drastic cuts of the 1960s. On 28 March 2018, DB Cargo's No. 60017 heads through Lincoln station on an empty tank working returning from Kingsbury to Humber.

Lincoln station provides an alternative route to the ECML for freight trains between Peterborough and Doncaster. On 28 March 2018, Freightliner's No. 66563 heads a container train from Leeds to Felixstowe.

These services had historically been routed via the Lincolnshire town of Grantham on the ECML. On 13 October 2016, No. 66501 *Japan 2001* heads south on the Leeds to Felixstowe liner.

First Hull Trains provide Grantham with several daily services between the Yorkshire city and London King's Cross. On 5 October 2016, their Class 180 unit, No. 180109, calls on a Hull to London service.

Other improvements to passenger services in the county mean that Gainsborough Central now enjoys an hourly service to Sheffield throughout the week. On 5 July 2019, No. 142067 has just terminated there.

Across the town at Gainsborough's Lea Road station, a new platform has just been opened for Sheffield and Doncaster-bound passengers. On 14 January 2020, East Midland Railway's (EMR) No. 156401 calls at the new platform on a Lincoln to Doncaster service.

GBRf also use this route via Gainsborough and Lincoln for a number of their freight services. On 8 March 2018, No. 66724 *Drax Power Station* passes Lea Road station on a working from Masborough, Rotherham, to Felixstowe.

At the southern end of the county, sister GBRf loco, No. 66749, is seen passing through Spalding station on 11 May 2018 on a working from Middleton Towers, near King's Lynn, to Goole.

The service from Nottingham to Skegness is a popular one, particularly during the holiday season, resulting in EMR units working in pairs on the busier services. On 7 July 2018, Nos 156497 and 156498 call at Wainfleet on a service for Skegness.

This view of Skegness station on 11 May 2018 gives a hint of a busier past. Today, it's rare to find more than one train at this seaside terminus. In this view, No. 158785 has just arrived on a service from Nottingham.

Peterborough

This important railway junction is at the south-eastern extremity of the rover ticket's area of validity. On 3 September 2019, one of LNER's recently introduced Azumas, No. 800106, calls at Peterborough on a service from London King's Cross to Leeds.

These new units have meant an end to LNER hiring of DB Cargo Class 90 electric locos to supplement their own loco fleet. On 30 May 2019, No. 90028 arrives on a King's Cross to Newark North Gate service. A train fault resulted in this service terminating here on that afternoon.

The iconic High Speed Trains (HST) have also been displaced on LNER services. On 31 October 2017, No. 43238 *National Railway Museum 40 Years 1975–2015* is seen calling at Peterborough on the rear of a London King's Cross service.

The hiring of additional HST power cars from EMR has also ceased. On 31 October 2017, power car No. 43075 is seen on the rear of a working from Leeds to King's Cross.

Peterborough is an important gateway for passengers travelling to and from East Anglia. Greater Anglia offer a service every two hours across the region from here to Ipswich via Bury St Edmunds. At the time of writing, new units are about to be phased in on these services. They are much needed, as this view of Greater Anglia's No. 153306 on 28 November 2019 demonstrates. The fully loaded, single-car unit was to leave Peterborough with many passengers forced to stand for their journey.

Their two-car Class 170 units have been the regular traction on these Peterborough to Ipswich services. These, too, are being transferred away. On 6 February 2019, No. 170271 waits at Peterborough to return to Ipswich.

For many years the Class 365 units were the preferred traction on Great Northern's limited stop services between Peterborough and London King's Cross. Today, they are used on a few peak services only. On 11 May 2018, No. 365509 waits to form a London service.

These Great Northern services are now routed via St Pancras International rather than King's Cross. This enables through running across London, using Class 700 units. Most services operate from Peterborough through to Horsham in West Sussex. On 30 May 2019, twelve-car unit No. 700115 is waiting to leave on a service to the Sussex town.

CrossCountry Trains operate an east to west service linking Peterborough with Birmingham New Street to the west and Stansted Airport to the South East. On 27 April 2016, No. 170106 calls on a service from Stansted to Birmingham New Street.

Most of the freight traffic through Peterborough takes the route to and from East Anglia, via March and Ely. One long-standing DB Cargo service that uses the southern end of the ECML is the delivery of Plasmor blocks from Yorkshire to the south. On 28 November 2019, No. 66135 is in charge of the northbound empties working from Bow in East London to Heck, near Goole.

The main line through Peterborough has long been associated with the iconic Flying Scotsman brand. LNER loco No. 91101 *Flying Scotsman* has carried its name for many years, although, in common with the rest of the class, its days are numbered. On 17 June 2015, the loco propels a London service away from Peterborough.

The use of Class 67 'Thunderbird' locos to rescue these LNER services are also numbered as a result. On 30 May 2019, No. 67006 *Royal Sovereign* speeds through Peterborough to carry out a rescue mission at Grantham.

Leicester

The city of Leicester sits at an important crossroads linking the Midland Main Line heading north to south with the cross-country artery between Birmingham and Peterborough to the west and east. On 8 October 2019, the depot is home to two displaced Class 90s, Nos 91117 and 91120. They already carry Europhoenix livery, ahead of a new life abroad.

The depot at Leicester can be seen from the north end of the station's platforms. Over the last few years a variety of loco classes have been in residence. On 14 December 2018, the line-up included, from left to right, No. 37608 *Andromeda*, No. 50008 *Thunderer*, and Nos 56091, 37503, 56060 and 33053.

Locos resident in the depot area are often confined to shunting moves within the confines of the yard. This is the case on 29 July 2019 when Class 33 loco No. 33053 is in charge of the movement of two barrier coaches.

On 26 October 2019, No. 37905 stands alongside No. 37601 on the depot's fuel point. Loco No. 37905 was newly released from English Electric as D6836 in April 1963, while No. 37601 is two years older. It was released as D6705 in January 1961.

The quarry at Mountsorrel, a few miles north of Leicester, is an important customer of the freight operators, including Direct Rail Services. Their infrastructure working from Crewe is seen passing through the station behind No. 68003 *Astute* on 8 June 2016.

The empty wagons are seen again on 14 January 2020. This time the traction is Class 66 loco No. 66422. After loading, these trains leave Mountsorrel and reach Crewe via Burton on Trent, avoiding Leicester.

Most of the stone from the quarry at Mountsorrel that is regularly despatched to Elstow, just south of Bedford, is in the hands of DB Cargo. On 8 October 2019 the empties are seen passing through Leicester behind No. 66060.

Another long-standing flow through Leicester is the steel traffic between Corby and Margam in South Wales. On 13 October 2016, No. 66176 passes the depot area and approaches the station with the empties returning to South Wales.

The cross-country route to and from Peterborough and East Anglia is an important route for container trains serving the port of Felixstowe. On 7 August 2019 Freightliner's No. 66544 heads north through Leicester station, working from Lawley Street in Birmingham to Felixstowe.

A few weeks later, on 15 October, it's the turn of GB Railfreight's No. 66711 *Sence* to head north on a container train, this time from the West Midlands terminal at Birch Coppice. It is seen waiting on the station's goods loop for the signal to proceed on the bi-directional line towards Syston. Once there, it will regain the double track line to Peterborough and across East Anglia to Felixstowe.

A number of workings to and from Brush's workshops at Loughborough pass through Leicester station. On 31 January 2017, London Midland's Class 170 unit No. 170501 heads from Tyseley, in Birmingham, to the workshops at Brush.

Another Loughborough move on 13 March 2017 brings a pair of GBRf locos to Leicester. Their Class 73 loco, No. 73961 *Alison*, is dragging Caledonian Sleeper-liveried No. 92023 to the works for attention.

Market Harborough to Bedford

The East Midlands Rover ticket covers the 50-or-so miles of the Midland Main Line (MML) south of Leicester as far as Bedford. On 7 June 2018, HST power car No. 43059 leads an EMR (or East Midlands Trains, as they were known then), through Market Harborough.

This section of the MML is often used for Network Rail Test Trains between their base at Derby and the former Southern Region of the UK network. On 13 October 2015, GBRf's No. 73212 *Fiona* is seen passing Market Harborough on the rear of a Derby return working from the yard at Tonbridge in Kent.

The former Grand Central HST power cars have since been used by EMR, including one early evening diagram from London St Pancras International to Corby. On 16 August 2019, No. 43468 is waiting departure from Kettering on the 17.46 service to Corby.

One of the longest distances, if not the longest, for any freight train is the Colas Rail service from Oxwellmains, near Dunbar in Scotland, to West Thurrock, near Grays in Essex. On 3 September 2019, No. 70814 approaches Kettering on the southbound loaded working for British building materials company Tarmac.

In 2016, the same company, Tarmac, awarded Freightliner the contract for rail movements from its site at Tunstead in Derbyshire. On 7 August 2019, No. 66605 waits at the signal in Kettering station in order to continue its service south on its journey to West Thurrock.

The five-car Meridians are the staple diet of EMR's stopping services on this stretch of the MML, with hourly services from London to both Corby and Nottingham. On 3 August 2018, No. 222016 calls at Wellingborough on a northbound service.

The line is serviced by Rail Head Treatment Trains (RHTT) during the leaf fall season. These workings operate in a top'n'tail mode from Toton as far south as West Hampstead. On 14 November 2016, the working was in the hands of DB Cargo's No. 67002. The Class 67 was leading on this southbound working through Wellingborough. Class 66 loco No. 66140 is on the rear.

On 6 September 2019, Wellingborough is again the location of this more unusual move. With Europhoenix Class 37 No. 37608 out of sight at the front, Crossrail unit No. 345066 is being taken to their depot at Old Oak in West London.

Another long-distance freight service that uses this stretch of the Midland Main Line is the Freightliner working from Moreton-on-Lugg, on the Welsh Border, to the Hertfordshire terminal at Radlett adjacent to the MML. On 14 January 2020, Freightliner's No. 66613 approaches Bedford station on the last leg of the inbound journey to Radlett.

On 2 March 2017, GBRf's No. 66715 *Valour* is seen approaching the same platform with a service from its yard at Wellingborough to the terminal at Elstow, a couple of miles south of here. The Bromham Road bridge in the background is one of the last to be raised in readiness for the Midland Main Line electrification to Kettering and Corby.

At the time of writing Bedford remains the northern limit of the electrified services, currently operated by Thameslink. The Thameslink service from Bedford through Central London to Brighton was in the hands of Class 319 units when this photo was taken on 1 December 2015. The unit, No. 319442, has just terminated on a service from Brighton.

On 26 April 2017, London Midland's two-car unit, No. 150109, waits in the bay platform at Bedford. It will shortly form a service on the Marston Vale branch to Bletchley. Appropriately, this photo completes our journey around the area covered by the East Midlands Rover ticket.